The ABC's of Uncivil Behavior in the Classroom

A Cautionary Tale of Draggles and Wowzers

Céleste Grimard & Michel Cossette

Céleste Grimard & Michel Cossette

Copyright © 2016

Céleste Grimard & Michel Cossette, Canada

All rights reserved. All materials on these pages are copyrighted by Céleste Grimard and Michel Cossette. Reproduction, modification, storage of all or a part of this book in a retrieval system or retransmission, in any form or by any means, electronic, mechanical or otherwise is strictly prohibited without prior written permission from the authors.

ISBN-13: 978-1537647302
CreateSpace, North Charleston, USA

This book is fictional in nature. Any resemblance to individuals or events is coincidental.

Céleste Grimard illustrated this book.

This book is available in French as *L'ABC des comportements (non) civils en classe*.

ACKNOWLEDGMENTS

We thank Anne Bourhis, Jack Ito, and Janice Foley for their helpful comments and suggestions on earlier drafts of this book. We also thank our former students, all of whom have taught us to become creative instructors.

Céleste Grimard & Michel Cossette

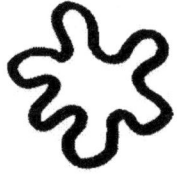
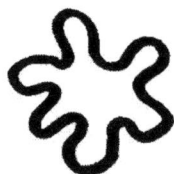

ONCE UPON A TIME, not so long ago and not too far away, in Classroom on Planet Draggle, a motley crew of Draggles had assembled. The continuity of their species depended on all young Draggles fulfilling their destiny: becoming Draggle Leaders in their personal and professional lives. To do so, they needed to learn stuff that could only be learned in Classroom where the latest scientific research is presented. But, Draggles were dragging themselves to Classroom and slacking off once they got there. They didn't seem to want to learn to become Draggle Leaders. They figured that they knew what they had to know, and that life would go on as it always had on Planet Draggle. Who cares about research evidence anyhow? Nothing new under the suns.

The ABC's of Uncivil Behavior in the Classroom

WOWZERS FROM PLANET WOWZIE, a nearby planet in the same galaxy as Planet Draggle, were eyeing all that was taking place on Planet Draggle through their space-time flex device. Wowzers are naturally ingenious and excited to learn more about themselves and others. They love learning about the worlds around them, and they pride themselves on making decisions based on research evidence. They also yearned to invite Planet Draggle to participate in an interplanetary federation.

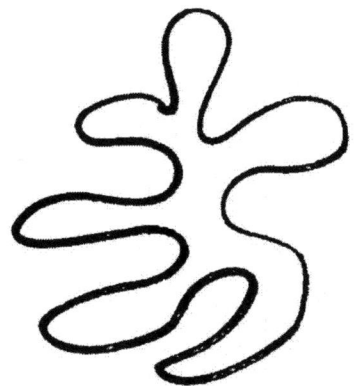

BESIDES, TOTALLY UNBEKNOWNST TO DRAGGLES, who didn't travel beyond their moons, Planet Draggle's oceans were the only source of high grade Zolto crystals in the galaxy. Wowzers spontaneously lost their eyesight during jon marr, their coming of age ritual, and they used synthetic Zolto crystals to recuperate their vision. Unfortunately, synthetic Zolto crystals, which were poor quality and in limited supply, were solely manufactured by the Gougees who took advantage of their monopoly by upping the price of Zolto crystals on a whim.

Wowzers wanted to be the first to contact Planet Draggle and, once the necessary period of familiarization had taken place, negotiate a favorable deal for Zolto crystals with their leaders. Draggles currently in Classroom would be the generation of leaders in place by the time negotiations start. So, naturally, Wowzers wanted to know more about these future leaders.

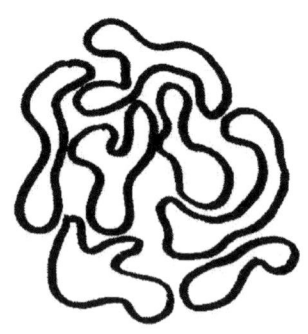

HOWEVER, the behavior they observed from a distance mystified Wowzers and suggested that Draggles might not be ready for first contact. So, Wowzers decided to study Draggles more closely by commissioning a small team of highly perceptive representatives to live incognito on Planet Draggle and observe Draggles in Classroom. After a reasonable period, these representatives returned to Planet Wowzie reporting that they had observed the following types of characters in Classroom.

Céleste Grimard & Michel Cossette

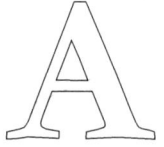

ALEX AWOL is rarely seen in Classroom. He's got his reasons, but he's missing out on a lot. He counts on his classmates to let him know what he missed, "if anything." And he messages Prof and asks, "Hey Yo! Are we doing anything important in class today?" Or, Alex AWOL shows up at Prof's office and commands Prof to go over anything that he might have missed. After all, he pays tuition fees, and Prof is paid to meet his needs. After midterm exams, even if there isn't a midterm break, Alex AWOL heads over to Planet O' Suns for a couple of weeks to recover from the stress of Classroom. "I'll ask my classmates to help me get caught up on anything important. And so what if I'm not around to contribute to their learning? Hey, that's not my responsibility. If I want to skip class, that's my business."

The ABC's of Uncivil Behavior in the Classroom

Where's Alex?
He's never here.

~

Who's Alex?

BUSY BOB is in Classroom, but he's juggling lots of balls. He takes a full load of classes, works 30 hours per week, he has an active social life, and he travels. "A guy's gotta relax, you know." Busy Bob scolds Prof for overloading him; he had three hours of work to do this week just for Prof's class. "That's majorly unfair," he says to Prof directly or to classmates while Prof is within earshot. And Busy Bob can be seen doing work for other classes in Prof's class. He has overloaded himself, but he expects to do well in all his classes even though he studies very little.

Busy Bob's second cousin, Lazy Lance, is a sluggish dude who wants a free ride – good marks for the least amount of work possible. Lazy Lance teams up with Busy Bob to persuade their classmates to join in harassing Prof to lower the workload. They tell Prof – and, in fact, every prof - that other profs give them half the amount of work to do, and Prof should too!

The ABC's of Uncivil Behavior in the Classroom

I ain't got time to study.
Gimme half the work and twice the marks.

Céleste Grimard & Michel Cossette

CHATTY CARL chats, chats, chats while Prof is talking, while classmates are answering questions, during exams, and, basically, whenever the urge strikes him. "I've got lots of important and clever stuff to say to whoever is sitting beside me, and I can't wait another minute." These side conversations distract other students and Prof, and they continue even if Prof is standing next to Chatty Carl. "So what if it bothers others, or Prof has to repeat instructions that I missed? My needs come first. And, if I think I have something urgent to say, then it's urgent. And how dare Prof call me out for it. I have the right to talk when I want. My parents paid my tuition fees! Talk to the hand!"

The ABC's of Uncivil Behavior in the Classroom

I talk even when I have nothing to say.

Céleste Grimard & Michel Cossette

DEBBIE DOWNER casts a shadow over everything that doesn't meet her expectations (and nothing is to her liking). The suns never shine on Debbie Downer who is constantly complaining, irritated, annoyed, moody, sensitive, negative, unhappy, blah... You can see the shadows expanding around her and her classmates who begin to feel miserable and question Classroom. Prof and the course become easy fodder for complaints as the ambience in Classroom blackens. Debbie Downer jumps at Prof's inevitable misstep, informs Prof's boss, and urges her classmates to submit negative evaluations of Prof's teaching. "If there's something to complain about, I'll complain. And, there's always something to complain about."

The ABC's of Uncivil Behavior in the Classroom

This sucks!
I hate it, and you should too!

EDEN EATER is hungry. She doesn't have a chance to eat before Classroom, or maybe she does, but she would rather nosh in Classroom. She's gobbling a meal of garlic sausage, fried onions, beans and curry rice and drowning it all in strong coffee. The whole class hears her crunching carrots and celery. There are spills, slurps, odors, spits, farts, burps, spits, drools. Eating with her mouth open. Sticky fingers. After 20 minutes, Eden Eater crushes the empty food and drink containers, casts them aside on a nearby table or the floor and pulls out her notebook. But, before she can concentrate on the class, she has to use the washroom. She steps on her classmates' stuff, saunters out Classroom, and leaves the door open to the hallway noises. Eden Eater has no idea that her classmates are disgusted by the spectacle, the sounds, and the odors.

The ABC's of Uncivil Behavior in the Classroom

Class time is nosh time!

Céleste Grimard & Michel Cossette

FASHION FANNIE is decked out. She has large hoop earrings, a perfect makeup job, crystals embedded in her long gel claws, and long hair that flows around her head one minute and is pulled into a high pony tail the next minute. Fashion Fannie spends her time in Classroom copiously brushing and flipping her hair, sometimes inspecting it for split ends. Her lipstick often needs to be refreshed. She carries her make-up kit in her designer satchel bag, which matches her knee high boots and her preppy hipster look. Who knows, she might be going to a fashion show or an upscale club after class. Fashion Fannie proudly displays the newest version of an array of electronic gadgets "A girl's gotta look good and have the best gear, you know." Naturally, learning activities that require handling paper or other materials are off-limits in case she wrecks her manicure.

"I could teach Prof a thing or two about style. Those pants are outta style, and that hair cut is from another century. Dowdy! You can't expect me to learn from someone who ain't got no style."

The ABC's of Uncivil Behavior in the Classroom

"And why are tuition and textbooks so expensive? I can barely afford my weekly spa treatments."

I grace this classroom with my presence.

Céleste Grimard & Michel Cossette

GERMY GEORGE should have stayed home. He's coughing and hacking and groaning in pain, and he's propelling thousands of germ particles and droplets into the air. His classmates have shifted their desks away from him and cringe when he accidentally touches their notebooks. Germy George prides himself on never missing Classroom, and he scoffs at the idea that he might pass on his illness to his classmates.

His friend, **MEDICAL MIRA**, does the opposite. She stays away from Classroom when she feels the slightest headache coming on. And she strategically obtains doctors' notes precisely when exams are being held or reports are due. This coincidental timing has been happening for the past three years! Is Medical Mira really sick? No one knows for sure, but her classmates see her shopping and lunching on the days she says she's sick. "Prof's gotta take it easy on me and make personal exceptions because that's what I want. If Prof doesn't accept my excuses, Prof is a cold hearted, rigid jerk."

The ABC's of Uncivil Behavior in the Classroom

Who me, sick?

Céleste Grimard & Michel Cossette

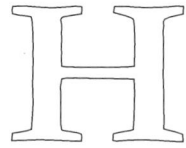

HARRY HOGGLER AND HARRY HAGGLER are twins.

Harry Hoggler hogs talk time in class. He's got lots to say, much of which is irrelevant. He drags on, and Prof can't cut in. Harry Hoggler's hand is always up. When Prof pretends to not see him, he just starts talking.

His twin, Harry Haggler, believes that all is negotiable: from the length of class to how groups are formed, what we do in Classroom, how learning is evaluated, how grades are attributed, when grades should be posted, and anything else under the suns. Absolutely everything's on the bargaining table, and he won't accept "no" as an answer. Midway through the semester, when Harry Haggler realizes how much work he has yet to do, he begins several rounds of negotiation with Prof to change the workload or, at the very least, his personal arrangements to accommodate his circumstances. "I didn't realize that I needed to read the textbook all along the semester, and now I have too much reading to do. Prof's gotta cut me some slack."

The ABC's of Uncivil Behavior in the Classroom

I push till I get my way, then I push some more!

Céleste Grimard & Michel Cossette

I

ILL-MANNERED AND VERY IMPOLITE IDA

never says *please, thank you, excuse me, I'm sorry, I made a mistake,* or anything else remotely resembling politeness. Ill-mannered and Very Impolite Ida and her cousin **RUDE RANDY** are a tag team combo who feel entitled to Everything. They won't lower themselves to show respect towards others, particularly Prof. They are right, and others are wrong. They spew forth vulgarities whenever they're expected to do some work. When Prof asked students to form groups, Ill-Mannered and Very Impolite Ida screeches, "This sucks!" loud enough for Prof to hear from the opposite side of the room. They leave garbage on their desks and the floor. Their written messages to Prof are void of courtesies and politeness. They call out Prof for errors and omissions (even *their* errors), and they order Prof to change their grades. When Prof tries to explain the grading process, they cut Prof off in mid-sentence and threaten to report Prof to 'someone in charge.' Listening and learning aren't their gig.

The ABC's of Uncivil Behavior in the Classroom

*Hey buddy! You screwed up!
Change my grade NOW! Or else!*

JUDGING JUDY acts like the judge and jury of all that happens in Classroom. In her mind, her opinion supersedes that of others, and she knows best. Instead of immersing herself in Classroom and trying to learn as much as possible, Judging Judy sits back and evaluates, judges and criticizes all that is said and done in Classroom. Judging Judy automatically sees the pimples, problems, and weaknesses in the course and the person who designed and delivered it (Prof). "I could do a way better job." And she complains when classes are too long or too short.

KARO BULLY, first cousin to Judging Judy and Debbie Downer, can't stand other students or any profs. She thinks that whoever has something to say in Classroom or in a workgroup is an idiot. Sarcasm and put-downs are Karo Bully's weapons of choice. "They're all a bunch of stupid jerks." Whenever someone is talking, Karo Bully rolls her eyes and sighs, "They're so annoyingly stupid!"

The ABC's of Uncivil Behavior in the Classroom

Classroom really sucks!

Céleste Grimard & Michel Cossette

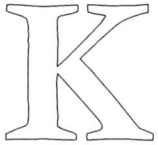

KARLA KERFUFFLE makes a fuss about anything and everything. She's super sensitive, and if Prof just looks at her the wrong way, there'll be hell to pay. Everything's a hassle, a problem, an issue, and an inconvenience. Karla Kerfuffle bangs her fists on her desk and glares at Prof when she learns that Prof is applying a previously agreed to late submission penalty to her report which was five days late. "Prof is so demanding and rigid. Cut me some slack!" Karla Kerfuffle argues for an extra point till she's purple in the face, not realizing that Prof may give her the point now just to get her off Prof's back but be extra vigilant in marking her next reports. Karla Kerfuffle may win the battle, but lose the war.

The ABC's of Uncivil Behavior in the Classroom

Prof's not fair!

Céleste Grimard & Michel Cossette

LATE AND LEAVING LARRY

never arrives to Classroom on time. "Prof's rule about waiting till break time to enter Classroom if we're late for class denies me my right to be in the room!" Late and Leaving Larry often leaves Classroom before the end of class. "It's only natural. The class doesn't fit my schedule, and I don't need to be here. If I miss anything, my classmates will tell me about it. Who cares if they need me for our group discussion? I don't!" Even when Prof is in the middle of a lecture, Late and Leaving Larry loudly packs up his stuff and walks out. So what if it makes noise and distracts his classmates! Apparently, he's got things to do, and he's got people to see that are so important that he needs to take time away from Classroom.

The ABC's of Uncivil Behavior in the Classroom

I got things to do and places to be.
Not here.

Céleste Grimard & Michel Cossette

MOOCHING MATT is a slacker. "Give me your notes. I don't take good notes." In fact, he doesn't take any notes during class. Sometimes, he begs Prof for notes ("my middle finger is sore from my accident five years ago"), but normally his classmates just copy their notes for him (reluctantly). He's the weak link on a team. An eternal procrastinator, he hopes that his team just ignores him and does his part of the work. He's gotten away with having several group projects written for him by faking serious personal issues at critical times or by massaging the egos of team members ("You're a much better writer than I am..."). He has even paid team members to do his part of a project. Eventually, this social loafing may catch up to him, but he's milking it as much as possible for as long as he can.

The ABC's of Uncivil Behavior in the Classroom

Mind doing my share of the project? Please?

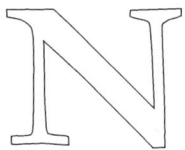

NEEDY NED needs Prof's constant attention and affirmation. He talks to Prof before class, during a break, while students are doing group work, and after class. He requests office visits, sends lots of written messages, and walks Prof to the office, all to make sure that he's on the right page. Needy Ned doesn't trust that he understands the lecture, course syllabus, or anything correctly. He needs Prof to pat him on the back and explain everything to him…one more time. And he wants to be Prof's friend.

The ABC's of Uncivil Behavior in the Classroom

Can I see you after every class?
And maybe walk home with you?

Céleste Grimard & Michel Cossette

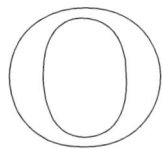

OPINIONATED OLGA could care less that research says x, y and z. If her experience differs from this research, then her personal view of the worlds, a sample of one, is what matters. If she thinks that 1 + 1 = 3, then she'll argue that she's right till others give in just to shut her up. "I already know everything that I need to know; why do I need to come to Classroom? I'm right, and everyone else is an idiot. If you don't share my opinion, then you've got some screws loose. Don't argue with me; you'll lose. Let me set you straight on things." Opinionated Olga thinks nothing of calling out Prof on so-called errors or challenging Prof on topics that are way off the subject at hand. "Planet Draggle isn't an oblate spheroid; it's round. Perfectly round. I saw it in a cartoon."

The ABC's of Uncivil Behavior in the Classroom

*Why do I need to be here?
I know everything already.
Just ask me.*

Céleste Grimard & Michel Cossette

PLAGIARIZING PAT loves what she reads so much that she writes it all down – word for word, or she changes a word here and there – and then signs her name to it. She thinks that Prof has so many reports to read that her "bit of using the same words" won't be detected or won't matter. Plagiarizing Pat thinks that Classroom's zero-tolerance plagiarism policy doesn't apply to her. When confronted, she replies that she has a perfect memory, that she didn't realize that she was plagiarizing, that Prof authorized it, that Prof's instruction weren't clear, that she simply forgot to insert quotation marks, or that she only plagiarized a little bit. "Give me a break. It wasn't intentional. Besides, isn't using someone else's words the greatest form of flattery? And, how dare you accuse me of plagiarism? You're really stressing me out. And, you're tarnishing my reputation by accusing me of plagiarism. Don't make such a big deal about it."

The ABC's of Uncivil Behavior in the Classroom

Who me? Plagiarize?

Céleste Grimard & Michel Cossette

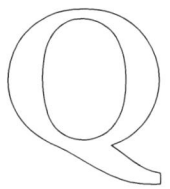

QUIZMASTER QUENTIN always finds ways to cheat on exams. He thinks that cheating is creativity in action, and he's a creative kind of guy. His go-to strategies: writing notes on his water bottle label, getting permission to use the toilet and, while there, consulting the notes that he stashed in a bag behind the toilet, using an ear plug or visors with built-in cameras, writing notes on his hat, putting notes in his pencil case, sending signals to others by coughing or by batting his eyelashes, passing notes with another student, and even glancing at a classmate's exam. "Hey, you gotta cheat to get ahead in this world; might as well get started now."

The ABC's of Uncivil Behavior in the Classroom

What's wrong with a little peak?

RUDE RANDY, whom we've already met, is someone who simply doesn't realize that he can get further by being polite, and that we catch more flies with honey than with vinegar. He is inattentive when Prof talks to him (sometimes interrupting, sometimes checking messages on his communication device, sometimes rolling his eyes and looking disgusted, and sometimes even walking away). But, when he has demands, Rude Randy is in Prof's face with his claws waving fiercely. He argues his point till Prof gives up, gives in, and silently retreats from the room. "Prof, you might call me aggressive, but I'm just standing up for myself. And, if you'd just shut up, you'd hear me better."

The ABC's of Uncivil Behavior in the Classroom

I could care less about what you're saying.

S

SIDETRACKER SUSAN is not on topic. Prof is talking about X, but Sidetracker Susan insists that Prof answer a question about Y. While her classmates are doing a group exercise on Z, Sidetracker Susan wants to talk to Prof about her term paper. She ignores Prof's encouragements to discuss this after class or make an office appointment. In fact, Sidetracker Susan is annoyed that Prof won't answer her questions on the spot. "What poor service. I'm the customer after all, and I want the answer to my question NOW while I'm thinking about it. I can't wait till the end of class. Who cares if it distracts other students or Prof?"

The ABC's of Uncivil Behavior in the Classroom

I don't care if I'm off topic.

Céleste Grimard & Michel Cossette

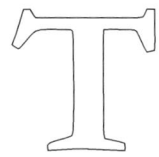

TEXTING TOMMY is constantly using some kind of electronic device, despite Prof's rules that communication devices and other technology not be used in Classroom. "Prof's so uptight. Prof has to get with technology." When Prof reminds Texting Tommy to put away his communication device, he puts it on his lap or the inside edge of his bag, and he continues texting. Texting Tommy doesn't realize that Prof sees this *lap texting*. Texting Tommy also enjoys checking written messages, watching movies, listening to music, and doing personal Dragglenet searches during class. Texting Tommy is in Classroom, but not *in* Classroom. When other students see that Texting Tommy is distracted by his devices, they take out their devices too. Classroom becomes a live *whack-a-mole* game. Who will Prof catch texting next? How many times can Prof say, "Put away your communication device!" in one class?

The ABC's of Uncivil Behavior in the Classroom

*I've got urgent texting to do.
Don't interfere with my texting!*

Céleste Grimard & Michel Cossette

U MUST ENTERTAIN ME UMA is

a passive, dependent learner. She expects Prof to be her source of motivation and inspiration because she's unable to motivate herself. U Must Entertain Me Uma expects Prof to entertain, amuse, charm, and stimulate her. "It's Prof's job to make me feel special and excited. If I'm bored, it's Prof's fault." She doesn't realize that boring people are easily bored. Furthermore, she rarely does the readings or takes notes. "Prof should do the readings for us, tell us what's important to know for exams, and share the slides with us. I don't have time to read and sort through what's important or not. And why should I have to take notes? That's Prof's job."

U Must Entertain Me Uma doesn't take responsibility for her learning or contribute to others' learning. She refuses to get involved in active learning activities because she considers Prof to be the only source of learning. What other students say is irrelevant. "If Prof doesn't tell me what I learned in a neatly packaged entertaining lecture with handouts, then I've learned nothing."

I'm bored. Please entertain me.
Your job is to entertain me.

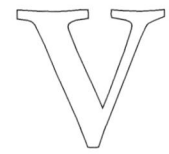

VOW OF SILENCE VIVIANE

says and does nothing, even if there are marks for class participation. Prof only hears from her if she gets a poor grade for participation. "You gotta give me full marks for participation. I was always in Classroom; you saw me. And, anyhow, I participated; I just didn't *say* nothing. Besides, you can't force me to talk, and you can't penalize me for not talking." Vow of Silence Viviane ignores even nonthreatening opportunities to contribute her perspective. She sits silently, sometimes transfixed on her computer screen, sometimes totally ignoring what is happening in Classroom. A bump on a log.

Viviane's friend, **STANDOUT STAN**, is her polar opposite. He loves to be the centre of attention, and he takes advantage of situations to make himself look good. Stan loves to give presentations on group projects, knowing that observers assume the presenter had greater input than others.

The ABC's of Uncivil Behavior in the Classroom

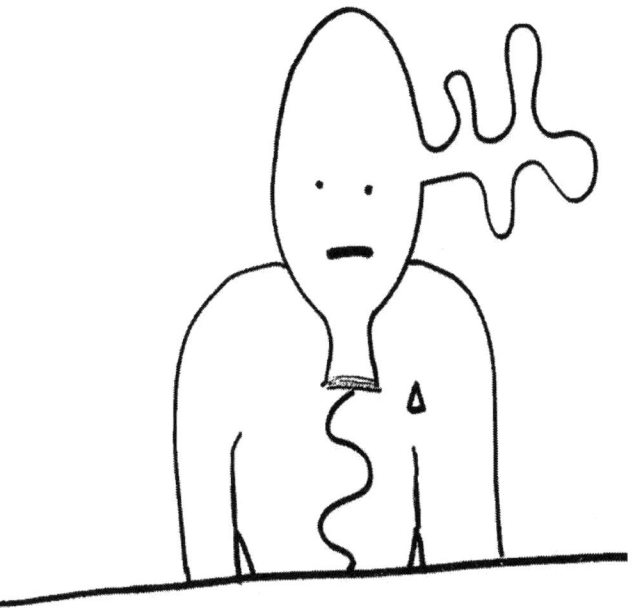

I ain't got nothin' to say, and you can't make me talk. Talking is YOUR job.

Céleste Grimard & Michel Cossette

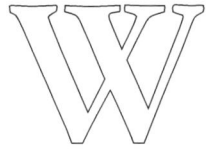

WOEFULLY UNPREPARED

WILLIAM doesn't come to Classroom prepared, and he has trouble contributing to group discussions. Before arriving at Classroom, he quickly highlights some lines on a few pages to give the impression that he has read the book. He tries to hide his lack of preparation, especially when Prof is nearby, by studying random notes from another class or by intensely examining pages in his textbook. He especially avoids eye contact with Prof. Sometimes he says whatever's on his mind that may be generally related to the discussion at hand, thinking that Prof will value this contribution as much as a precise contribution that reflects much preparation. "Prof shouldn't expect me to do any work before coming to Classroom. It's unrealistic. Anyhow, I can just fake it. Prof will never know that I did diddly-squat."

The ABC's of Uncivil Behavior in the Classroom

Homework? What homework?
I'll just pretend to be studying my notes.

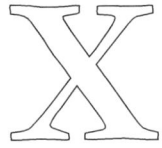

X-PERT XAVIER, like Opinionated Olga, is not shy about sharing what he thinks. But, X-pert Xavier sees himself and his generation as experts, and others as out-of-date or old fashioned. He could be completely wrong about something, but he doesn't accept other viewpoints, especially those of old fogies like Prof. "Prof lives in an Ivory Tower and is old and out of touch. I know what happens on the Street."

His cousin, **LUNA FOGGY,** pays just a little attention to the readings, classes, and assignments. "That's more than enough to get by. After all, Classroom has nothing to do with what happens in the Real World. Real leaders don't do what we're learning in Classroom. Besides, other profs say the opposite of what you're saying. Prof, you're wrong and outta touch and so are your expectations!"

Oops! When it's time to hand in an assignment, Luna Foggy says that she worked many hours on her assignment and that, because of this, she should automatically get a good grade. But, Luna Foggy's work is superficial, missing nuances, depth, and evidence of learning. Her explanations to Late and Leaving Larry are incomplete and incorrect, leaving him mad at Prof.

I already know all there is to know.
I've been schooled in the Real World.
And don't expect me to explain myself.

Céleste Grimard & Michel Cossette

YELLING YOLANDA is a raging bully who wants to have her way every day. She raises her voice anytime she feels like it; for example, when she doesn't like her grade on an exam or a report, when she doesn't feel like working on an group exercise in Classroom, and, especially, if Prof challenges her disruptive behavior. If Yelling Yolanda is afraid that she'll get a poor grade in the class, she pre-emptively visits Prof's boss, starts crying, and declares herself a helpless victim of Prof's oppressive and intimidating treatment. "I'm being targeted by Prof for no good reason." She knows that accusing Prof of misbehavior takes attention away from her own behavior.

The ABC's of Uncivil Behavior in the Classroom

I hate this, and it's your fault!

Similarly, her friend, **PETER PROF IS RESPONSIBLE AND GUILTY FOR ANY AND ALL EVILS IN THIS WORLD**, readily points his finger at Prof if he doesn't succeed in Classroom according to his personal definition of success. "It's not up to me to read Prof's instructions on how to do a report or what to study or to ask Prof questions about that stuff; that's Prof's job! That's what Prof's paid for! If I got it wrong, obviously the instructions weren't clear. Or Prof's a hard marker. Where did Prof get this grade from anyhow?" When Peter Prof Is Responsible and Guilty For Any And All Evils In This World asks Prof to explain his assignment's poor grade, his voice cracks, and he says that he has "never ever" received grades lower than 100%, hoping that Prof will give in and adjust his grade. But, this is the same story that he tells other profs. He hides the fact that his grade in Classroom is similar to what he usually receives in other classes. And when Peter Prof Is Responsible and Guilty For Any And All Evils In This World doesn't receive his bursary or grant, it's Prof's fault. "Prof must have told them lies about me! Jerk!"

The ABC's of Uncivil Behavior in the Classroom

Prof is responsible for all that is bad in this world — and my poor grades.

Céleste Grimard & Michel Cossette

Z

ZZZZ ZOË catches up on her sleep during class. "I'm tired, and Classroom is just plain boring!" Sometimes, Zzzz Zoë and her brother, **ZZZZ ZANE**, wear hats in a way that hides their eyes and makes it look like they're studying their notes. When Prof asks them a question, they are mortified that they would be put on the spot like that. "We need our zzzz's, and Prof should respect that. We're just resting our eyes after all."

The ABC's of Uncivil Behavior in the Classroom

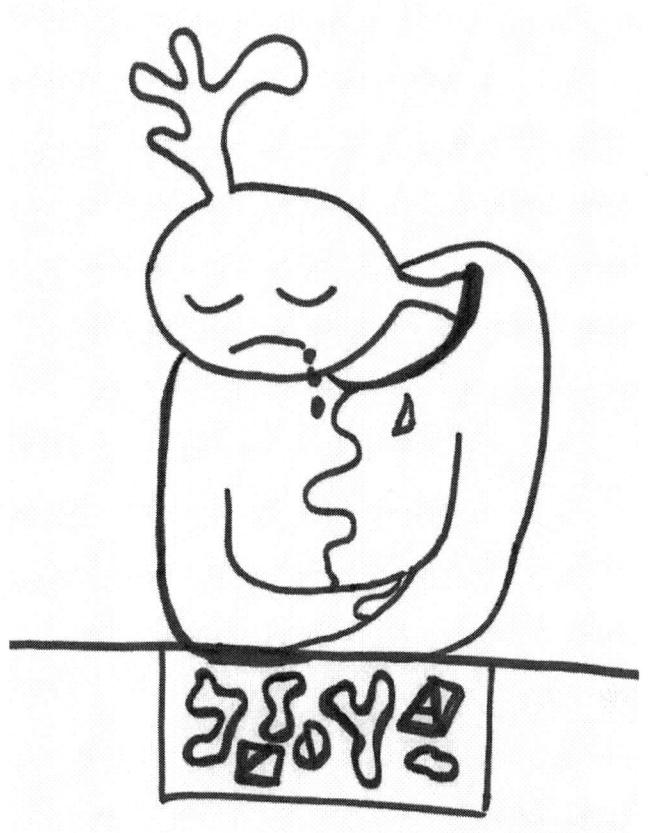

*I'm reflecting on my notes.
Don't hassle me.*

Céleste Grimard & Michel Cossette

WOWZERS!

The incognito team of highly perceptive representatives from Planet Wowzer confirmed what they had seen through their space-time flex device. Draggles everywhere are dragging themselves down, feeling stressed, bored or angry, focusing on themselves and being insensitive to others, and doing everything but learning to become leaders.

The ABC's of Uncivil Behavior in the Classroom

Do we look like leaders or what?

Céleste Grimard & Michel Cossette

WOWZERS CAN'T BELIEVE THIS CAST OF CHARACTERS!

Alex AWOL
Busy Bob and Lazy Lance
Chatty Carl
Debbie Downer
Eden Eater
Fashion Fannie
Germy George and Medical Mira
Harry Hoggler and Harry Haggler
Ill-Mannered and Very Impolite Ida
Judging Judy and Karo Bully
Karla Kerfuffle
Late and Leaving Larry
Mooching Matt
Needy Ned
Opinionated Olga
Plagiarizing Pat
Quizmaster Quentin
Rude Randy
Sidetracker Susan
Texting Tommy
U Must Entertain Me Uma
Vow of Silence Viviane and Standout Stan
Woefully Unprepared William
X-Pert Xavier and Luna Foggy
Yelling Yolanda and Peter Prof Is Responsible and Guilty For Any And All Evils In This World
Zzzz Zoë and Zzzz Zane

The ABC's of Uncivil Behavior in the Classroom

Draggles are the mirror images of Wowzers:
Alex Always in Class and Alert
Bob Busy but Well Organized and Accountable
Considerate Carl
Debbie Ray of Sunshine
Eden Eating and Visiting the Washroom Before Class
Fannie Focused on Learning
George Gets Well at Home and Medical Mira Never Fakes Illnesses to Get Out of Work
Harry Happy to Share Talk Time and Honor Expectations
Ida Illustratively Super Polite, Civil, and Respectful
Judy Appreciative and Bright Side Thinker
Calm and Accepting Karla
Larry in Classroom for the Full Class
Matt Hard Worker Who Does His Share (and More)
Ned Independent but Interdependent in a Team Setting
Olga Open to Other Perspectives
Pat Pens her own Work
Honest Quentin who Abhors Cheating
Respectful Randy
Stay on the Subject at Hand Susan
Tuck Away Technology During Class Tommy
Uma Self-Directed and Self-Motivated Learner
Vocal Participative Viviane and Shared Spotlight Stan Prepared for Class William
Xavier Open to Other Viewpoints
Courteous and Mature Yolanda
Wide Awake and Ready to Learn Zoë and Zane

Céleste Grimard & Michel Cossette

AFTER HEARING THEIR REPRESENTATIVES' REPORT,

Wowzer leaders reflected on their next course of action. Which of the Draggle characters would be the best negotiators? Wowzers weren't so sure that any Draggles were ready for first contact, or that they could reasonably negotiate a deal for Zolto crystals.

Through much investigation over millennia, Wowzers learned that civility and leadership go hand in hand. Civility is a basic requirement of leadership. No civility means no leadership. Wowzers also learned that behavior in one setting reflects behavior in other settings. So a Draggle who acts like a jerk in Classroom will likely do the same outside of Classroom. And, just as Wowzer Yolanda is courteous and mature in Classroom, she is courteous and mature in life. A duck is a duck is a duck. But, what should Wowzers do?

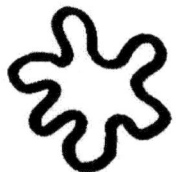

SHOULD WOWZERS SIMPLY BEAM DOWN and grab the Zolto crystals?

Planet Draggle would be easy to invade: Draggles seem to be so focused on themselves and scratching their little sores that they may not notice Wowzers descending upon and visiting their planet's oceans, absorbing their Zolto crystals. But that would involve stealing resources, and Wowzers would never do to Draggles what they wouldn't want done to themselves (except a bit of incognito visiting, of course).

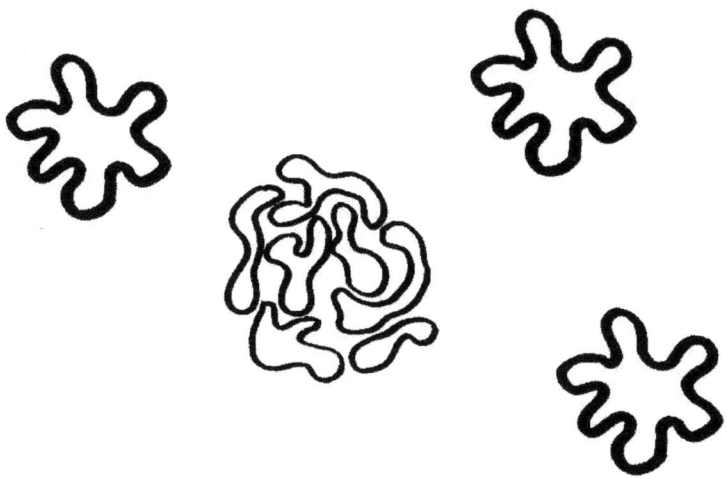

Céleste Grimard & Michel Cossette

PERHAPS, WOWZERS COULD INFILTRATE DRAGGLE SOCIETY

and, through coaching and modelling, gradually transform how they interact with each other without Draggles realizing that they are under alien influence (however constructive). But that would entail subliminally influencing another species, which is inconsistent with Wowzers' grand vision of interplanetary peace, love and understanding.

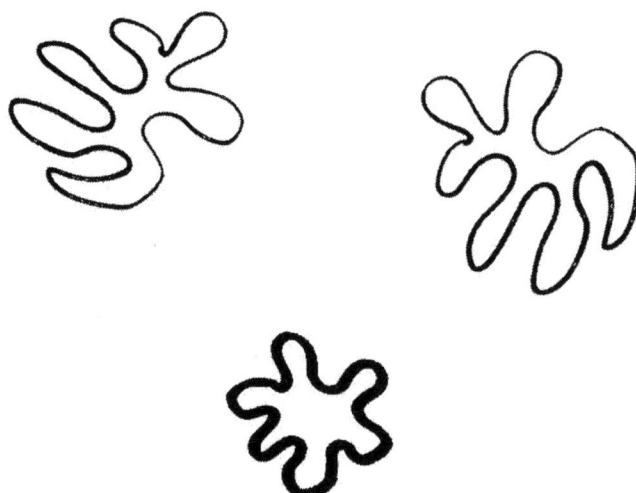

The ABC's of Uncivil Behavior in the Classroom

ANOTHER OPTION WOULD BE TO SEND PLANET WOWZIE'S BEST REPRESENTATIVES to Planet Draggle to meet with its best representatives. Over time, any initial fear might transform into cautious acceptance as Wowzers share their technology with Draggles. But would this take too much time?

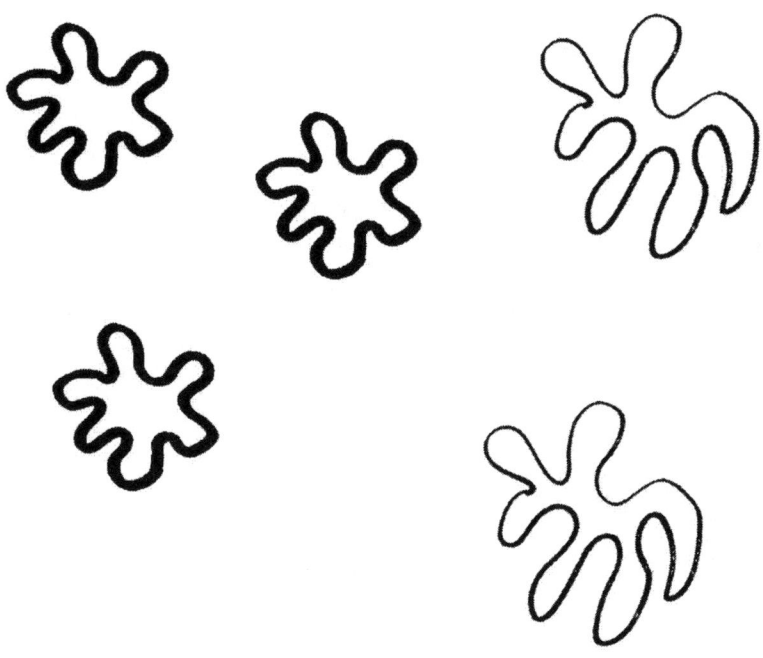

Céleste Grimard & Michel Cossette

HOW ABOUT DESCENDING UPON PLANET DRAGGLE WITH A FLEET OF 11,111 SHIPS flashing their friendship lights and 111,111 Wowzers extending tentacles of peace while beaming down? Draggles may misinterpret this as an alien invasion, which could generate shock, fear and aggression. After all, the unknown, especially in large quantities, can be overwhelming. But in tiny doses, the unknown may be more palatable. What should Wowzers do?

The ABC's of Uncivil Behavior in the Classroom

Céleste Grimard & Michel Cossette

REFLECTION QUESTIONS

1. What alternative endings do you envision for this tale? If you were a Wowzer, what would you do?
2. Who would you consider to be:
   a. Planet Wowzie's best representatives to Planet Draggle? Why?
   b. Planet Draggle's best representatives? Why?
3. How might Draggle ways become obstacles in interactions with Wowzers, particularly in negotiating for Zolto crystals?
4. Of the Draggle ways, which do you consider to be the five worst? Why?
5. How would you define civility? Incivility?
6. If you had to order the Draggle ways on a scale from the most civil to the least civil, how would your continuum look?
7. What other Draggle ways have you observed that aren't included in this tale (for example, chewing gum, shaming or ostracizing another student)?
8. How do Draggle ways harm the learning environment?
9. What is your usual reaction to Draggle ways?
10. Which five Draggles would you least want to work with on a team? Why?

11. Which Draggles would be most open to changing their ways?
12. What five Draggle ways do you typically see in the classroom?
13. Which five Wowzers would you would most want to have on your team? Why? Provide concrete examples of their behaviors.
14. What can students do to discourage Draggle ways and encourage Wowzer behaviors?
15. What will you personally do to discourage Draggle ways and encourage Wowzer behaviors in other students?
16. Which Draggle ways and which Wowzer behaviors represent what you do in the classroom?
17. What will you do differently to:
    a. Eliminate your Draggle ways?
    b. Engage in Wowzer behaviors so that you make a positive contribution to the classroom?
18. What can Prof do to discourage Draggle ways and encourage Wowzer behaviors?
19. Do you think that even mild versions of Draggle behaviors should be called out, because small problems become big problems (the equivalent of 'death by a thousand cuts')? Or… not?

20. Which Draggle ways seem to overlap or fit together well and are likely to form an alliance? Which are more likely to be in conflict?
21. Can students display both Draggle and Wowzer behaviors?
22. Why do students behave in Draggle ways? What might cause students to engage in Draggle ways?
23. What underlying themes can you see in the Draggle ways?
24. Which quotations in the Deep Thoughts section most appeal to you? Why?

The ABC's of Uncivil Behavior in the Classroom

ARE YOU A DRAGGLE OR A WOWZER?

We present these Draggle ways in their extreme caricatured forms as a way of clearly illustrating different types of incivility for the sake of discussion. Almost everyone has displayed one or more of these behaviors to some degree. (We have!) The first step to changing your Draggle ways is to figure out what you're doing that isn't working for you or others. You can do this by asking yourself four sets of questions:

1. How do others react to me? Are they happy to see me? Or do they seem to avoid me? Are they simply polite, engaging solely in small talk? Are they itching to get away?
2. What feedback about my behavior have others given me? (Sometimes, we fool ourselves. We just don't have any idea that we're screwing up, and we need direct feedback from someone, no matter how much it stings. Asking for and receiving honest feedback from others can be the best thing that ever happened to you, however risky it might feel in the short-term. If you're doing something that's preventing you from getting the results you want, wouldn't you want to know?)

3. What's the impact of what I'm doing? Is it really working for me in the short term or the long term? What sort of relationships am I building with others? Am I growing as a person? Am I truly happy with what I'm doing? Would I be embarrassed to have my behavior described on the front page of the newspaper?

4. What does my behavior in the classroom say about my overall approach to life? For example, do I try to give a little (or nothing at all) but get a lot? Do I play the blame and complain game? Do I tend to feel cheated or misunderstood by others? Am I often in a bad mood? Do I wait for others to take the lead and feel frustrated when nothing happens? Am I mainly focused on myself and what I want, possibly at the expense of others?

LOOK FOR PATTERNS IN YOUR ANSWERS

Are you behaving more like a Draggle or a Wowzer? Are you a civil person? If you're not getting the results you want, if you're feeling crappy about constantly being embroiled in conflict, or if you're not learning much, then these are signs that what you're doing isn't working for you. Lots of people don't get to this stage of realization and discomfort. They would rather bury their head in the sand and avoid this business of trying change Draggle behaviors that feel comfortable but that are just plain ineffective. Congratulate yourself for making the effort to understand your behavior and your results!

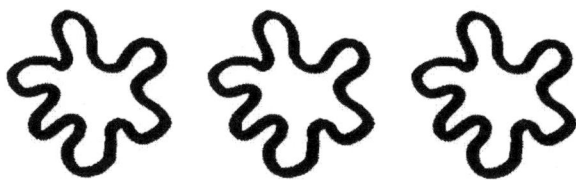

CHALLENGE YOUR DRAGGLE WAYS

Being a Draggle is no fun for anyone! Draggle ways bring everyone down and poison the learning environment. Draggles seem to lack awareness or consideration for how others see them; taking but not giving, focusing on what they want at others' expense, and being insensitive to others. In contrast, leaders act like Wowzers. Leaders, at the very least, are civil people. People listen to them and want to be around them because they feel respected. If you want to be respected, you've got to be civil. Here are some tips for becoming more civil:

1. **Take responsibility for what you do or don't do.** You're responsible for your behaviors. Whether you realize it or not, you have chosen your behaviors, and you can 'un-choose' them. You're not a puppet on a string. You can exercise self-discipline and self-control. It isn't necessary to express every thought, to fight every battle, or to react to everything that others do or don't do. YOU choose. You retain agency and the freedom to make your own choices and take responsibility for the results of your choices.

2. **Keep in mind that no one can hurt your feelings.** Negative feelings are signals that what you're doing or thinking isn't helping you meet your needs. Restructure (change) how you think about things, and you'll change how you feel. Two people can be in the same situation and interpret it differently. It's our interpretations of things that often get us into trouble, especially when we think that someone has intentionally tried to hurt us. Ask yourself if there are different ways to interpret a situation.

3. **Give people the benefit of the doubt.** Ask them what's going on. Don't automatically assume that someone's out to get you. They may have made a mistake unintentionally. You haven't walked a mile in their shoes. They may be going through a hard time personally or professionally, so their behavior may be out of whack. And, there may be a policy or other situational factors influencing their behavior. Making assumptions about why other people do things gets us into trouble. Besides, we're all human. No one's perfect. Holding on to resentments and anger hurts you more than other people.

4. **Communicate directly with the person involved.** Don't talk with everyone about the problem you're having with Person X; this makes you part of the problem, not the solution. Instead, choose the right moment, and talk directly with Person X. Calmly.

Share your observations, and then your interpretations. Try to agree on the facts, and be open to other interpretations. Take responsibility whenever you can. Don't cut others off or walk away in mid-sentence. Listen. Wait till they've finished saying what they have to say. Don't get angry, don't accuse, don't yell, don't be hostile, don't call people names, don't pout, don't threaten, don't be rude, don't guilt-trip, don't roll your eyes, don't point your finger, don't order, and don't push. That's not how you make friends and influence people. And, none of these behaviors are effective, at least in the long run. Someone might agree to your demands in the short term just to get you off their back but you lose their respect, and you lose the game in the long run. It's hard to repair a relationship that you've broken through your bad behavior.

5. **Be polite and respectful.** Courtesy doesn't take extra time or effort, and it allows others to see you as a reasonable person who is in control of yourself. Saying *please, thank you, sorry, excuse me* and other expressions of politeness are simple ways to show that you respect others. If you want others to respect you, you have to show them respect first.

6. **Get rid of your sense of entitlement.** It just gets in your way and makes people think that you haven't grown up yet. You are not the Center of the Universe. People do not exist to serve you. Don't think that everything has to be handed to you on a silver plate, or that everything has to go your way. Mature adults realize that they have rights AND responsibilities as do those around them. If your focus is on your rights and what's due to you, you'll likely trample on the rights of others because you'll see people as being in your way. You can't always get what you want, but you can try to get some of your needs met while respecting the rights of others to do the same.

7. **Put things in perspective.** Really now, how important is that extra point on your exam? Is it going to make a huge difference in your life? When you look back 10 or 20 years from now, what do you think will be most important to you? Are you willing to yell and scream while pushing for the extra point, but damage the relationship in the process? Sometimes, we get stuck in the rut of the moment, we ruminate, and we just can't see our way out of the mess we create for ourselves. But, things get better, and, in the long run, minor irritations are meaningless. Don't waste your time scratching little sores. Focus on what's really important.

8. **Be professional.** Ask yourself, "What would a professional, mature person do in this situation?" No Draggle behaviors, however justified in your mind, are what we see successful professionals doing. If you want to be a professional, start now, by acting in a mature, calm, considerate and reasonable manner.

9. **Be positive and agreeable.** If you have the choice between being positive and being negative (and, by the way, we all have this choice in every circumstance), why not be positive? Being negative hurts you, your reputation, your results, your relationships, and, yes, your body. It brings you down physically, mentally, socially, and spiritually. You probably don't realize how horrible you look to others when you're being a jerk. When you're behaving like a jerk to someone, they just want to be a jerk right back to you. Emotions are contagious and have a ripple effect on those around you. So, be aware of what you're projecting and radiating to others. Are you sapping them of energy, or are you helping others feel more energized?

10. **Use humor**, when appropriate, to help yourself deal with potentially embarrassing or difficult situations. This demonstrates your humanity, softens the tone of exchanges, and helps people save face. More importantly, learn to laugh at yourself, admit your errors, and be generous with others.

11. **Practice the Golden Rule "Do unto others as you would have them do unto you" and the Platinum Rule, "Treat others the way they want to be treated."** Civility means respecting others and regarding every person as being worthy of consideration, whether we like or agree with them. If everyone took responsibility for behaving in a civil manner, then we would create a civil society. Are you strengthening the goodwill that exists in this world, or are you the weak link?

12. **Focus on the positive things that others contribute, and show gratitude whenever possible.** As leadership expert Ken Blanchard suggests, "Catch people doing something right," and let them know that you appreciate them. It shows that you are a team player who works well with others rather than competing with them or focusing on their errors. Even people in positions of authority such as Prof need to feel that they are appreciated. We are all people who need people. When you disrespect or dismiss someone, you're telling them that they are of little worth to you. These undermining behaviors can destroy someone's sense of self-worth.

13. **Try to adopt a spirit of openness at all times.** Life is an amazing cornucopia of experiences and opportunities. There are different ways to learn, teach, and experience the world. You have found a way of being that's comfortable for you, but others also have their own perspectives. Trying to be flexible, stepping out of your comfort zone, and being open to other ways of being and doing things will help you grow as a person. It'll also help you become more creative when you're faced with new situations.

14. **Be a source of learning and light for others.** Try to become a "vessel of learning" and help others learn things through you. Being a good classmate means not only being a good example for others, but also taking the initiative to help those who may be having trouble learning.

15. **Be realistic and get organized.** Don't overload yourself. Figure out how to manage your time, your mood and yourself well, and do it. This is a basic skill for success at work, school, and home. Try to learn this lesson as early in life as possible. Procrastination is a dead end, a sure way to fail. You might be able to procrastinate and get by in the short term, but getting by isn't the same as succeeding. That rush that you get that spurs you to finish a report at the last minute is interpreted by your body as stress, and stress can do nasty things to your body (hypertension, fatigue, sleep disturbances, anxiety, digestion problems, etc.).

16. **Realize that learning is an investment that you make in yourself.** You're only hurting yourself by not studying or by minimizing how much time and effort you put into your classes. Make your classes your priority and study hard, and you'll like the results. You'll be proud of yourself!

The ABC's of Uncivil Behavior in the Classroom

DEEP THOUGHTS

"Whoever one is, and wherever one is, one is always in the wrong if one is rude."
— Maurice Baring

"Remember there's no such thing as a small act of kindness. Every act creates a ripple with no logical end."
— Scott Adams

"There is no beautifier of complexion, or form, or behavior, like the wish to scatter joy and not pain around us."
— Ralph Waldo Emerson

"Remember not only to say the right thing in the right place, but far more difficult still, to leave unsaid the wrong thing at the tempting moment."
— Benjamin Franklin

"This is the first test of a gentleman: his respect for those who can be of no possible value to him."
— William Lyon Phelps

"Whenever there is a human being, there is an opportunity for a kindness."
— Lucious Annaeus, *Seneca*

"Life is what our relationships make it. …Good relationships make our lives good; bad relationships make our lives bad….To learn how to be happy we must learn how to live well with others, and civility is a key to that."
—P.M. Forni, *Choosing Civility*

"Life is relational. Whether we like it or not, we are wax upon which other leave their mark. When someone sees us as a thing to use or abuse, that becomes part of who we are in our own eyes as well (self-esteem notwithstanding), When we are on the receiving end of an act of kindness, we feel validated. We translate that act into a very simple, very powerful unspoken message to ourselves: I am not alone, I have value and my life has meaning."
—P.M. Forni, *Choosing Civility*

The ABC's of Uncivil Behavior in the Classroom

"When the healthy pursuit of self-interest and self-realization turns into self-absorption, other people can lose their intrinsic value in our eyes and become mere means to the fulfillment of our needs and desires."
— P.M. Forni, *The Civility Solution*

"When you know you can do something, and you feel good about yourself, you do not have to devalue others."
— John Patrick Hickey, *Oops! Did I Really Post That*

"Wisdom tells us that the best time for silence is when we are mad or upset."
— John Patrick Hickey, *Oops! Did I Really Post That*

"You don't have to prove confidence; when you have it, it'll show. Real confidence is quiet, tactful, civil, and humble."
— Rosalinda Oropez Randall, *Don't Burp in the Boardroom: Your Guide to Handling Uncommonly Common Workplace Dilemmas*

"A talent for forgetting is necessary to maintain civility."
—Matthew De Abaitua, *If Then*

"When once the forms of civility are violated, there remains little hope of return to kindness or decency."
— Samuel Johnson

"The happiness of your life depends upon the quality of your thoughts."
— Marcus Aurelius

"Emotional competence implies we have a choice as to how we express our feelings."
— Dan Goleman

"We have a choice about how we behave, and that means we have the choice to opt for civility and grace."
— Dwight Currie

"Respecting the 'No' of another is one of the most elementary and significant rules of respect."
— P.M. Forni

"What is civility if not a constant awareness that no human encounter is without consequence?"
— P.M. Forni

The ABC's of Uncivil Behavior in the Classroom

"Manners are based on an ideal of empathy, of imagining the impact of one's own actions on others. They involve doing something for the sake of other people that is not obligatory and attracts no reward."
— Lynne Truss, *Talk to the Hand*

"The interesting thing is that, cut free from any sense of community, we are miserable and lonely as well as rude. This is an age of social autism, in which people just can't see the value of imagining their impact on others, and in which responsibility is always conveniently laid at other people's doors."
— Lynne Truss, *Talk to the Hand*

"Civility costs nothing, and buys everything."
— Mary Wortley Montagu

SUGGESTED READING

P.M. Forni, *Choosing Civility: The Twenty-five Rules of Considerate Conduct*

P.M. Forni, *The Civility Solution: What to do When People are Rude*

John Patrick Hickey, *Oops! Did I Really Post That*

M. Scott Peck, *A World Waiting to be Born: Search for Civility*

Rosalinda Oropez Randall, *Don't Burp in the Boardroom: Your Guide to Handling Uncommonly Common Workplace Dilemmas*

Lynne Truss, *Talk to the Hand*

The ABC's of Uncivil Behavior in the Classroom

Céleste Grimard & Michel Cossette

The ABC's of Uncivil Behavior in the Classroom

Are there any leaders on Planet Draggle? Wowzers from a nearby planet in the same galaxy as Planet Draggle hope to negotiate an interplanetary agreement with Draggles, but Draggles don't appear to be up to it. Their future leaders are an interesting assortment of characters who drag themselves to Classroom and slack off once they get there.

The ABC's of Uncivil Behavior in the Classroom is a colourful tale of memorable characters that illustrates what not to do in a classroom. It includes reflection questions and tips for becoming more civil. This fable is a fun way for students to learn about civility in the classroom (and in life!) and for instructors to get the message across that civility benefits everyone.

Céleste Grimard PhD is a professor at Université du Québec à Montréal. Michel Cossette is a professor at Hautes Études Commercial, also in Montréal, Canada.

Made in the USA
Columbia, SC
14 July 2018